World War I: The Western Front

Nicola Barber

First published by Hodder Wayland
338 Euston Road, London NW1 3BH, United Kingdom
Hodder Wayland is an imprint of Hodder Children's Books, a division of Hodder Headline Limited.
This edition published under license from Hodder Children's Books. All rights reserved.

Produced for Hodder Wayland by White-Thomson Publishing Ltd.
2/3 St. Andrew's Place, Lewes BN7 1UP, United Kingdom
Copyright © 2003 White-Thomson Publishing Ltd.

Editor: Anna Lee, Designer: Derek Lee, Consultant: Neil de Marco, Proofreader: Philippa Smith,
Photo researcher: Shelley Noronha (Glass Onion Pictures)

Published in the United States by Smart Apple Media
1980 Lookout Drive, North Mankato, Minnesota 56003

Library of Congress Cataloging-in-Publication Data

Barber, Nicola. World War I: the western front / by Nicola Barber.
p. cm. — (Questioning history)
Summary: Discusses the principal causes and events of World War I and considers what the outcome
might have been for the participants and subsequent history had different decisions been made at
crucial times before, during, and after the war. Includes bibliographical references and index.
ISBN 1-58340-268-3
1. World War, 1914–1918—Campaigns—Western Front—Juvenile literature. 2. World War,
1914–1918—Trench warfare—Juvenile literature. 3. Military weapons—History—20th century—
Juvenile literature. 4. Europe—Politics and government—1871–1918—Juvenile literature. [1. World
War, 1914–1918—Campaigns—Western Front. 2. World War, 1914–1918—Trench warfare. 3.
Europe—Politics and government—1871–1918. 4. Military weapons—History—20th century.]
I. Title. II. Series.

D530 .B25 2003   940.4'144—dc21   2002036590

9 8 7 6 5 4 3 2 1

Picture credits: AKG, 8, 17, 18, 22, 23, 24, 26, 31, 36, 38, 48, 57, 59; Camera Press, 21, 33; Hodder
Wayland Picture Library, 10, 30, 32, 43, 58; Mary Evans, 44, 49, 50; Peter Newark Military Pictures,
cover, 35, 54; Popperphoto, 6, 7, 15, 20, 28, 34, 42, 46, 52, 56; Topham, 13, 29, 39, 41; maps by The
Map Studio

CONTENTS

Going to War

ALLIANCES

When war broke out in 1914, a system of alliances between different countries ensured that the conflict quickly involved most of the major European powers. By 1914, the two main groupings were the Triple Alliance between Germany, Austria-Hungary, and Italy, and the Triple Entente between Britain, France, and Russia. But these alliances had their origins in events more than 40 years earlier.

In 1871, Prussia (a north German state) defeated France in the Franco-Prussian War. The end of the Franco-Prussian War also marked the unification of the separate German states into a single power, the German Empire. The war served to heighten tensions between France and its neighbor, but many other European states also began to look with some alarm at the new power in the center of Europe.

BELOW *Europe in 1914.*

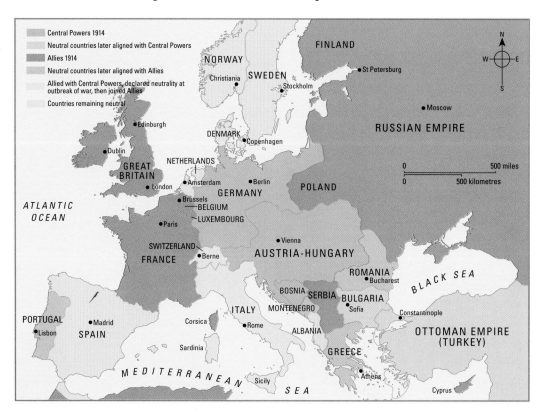

	Central Powers 1914
	Neutral countries later aligned with Central Powers
	Allies 1914
	Neutral countries later aligned with Allies
	Allied with Central Powers, declared neutrality at outbreak of war, then joined Allies
	Countries remaining neutral

FINLAND

NORWAY
Christiania
SWEDEN
Stockholm
St Petersburg

Moscow

RUSSIAN EMPIRE

Edinburgh
DENMARK
Copenhagen
Dublin
NETHERLANDS
GREAT
BRITAIN
London
Amsterdam
Berlin
GERMANY
POLAND
Brussels
BELGIUM
LUXEMBOURG
Paris
Vienna
SWITZERLAND
FRANCE
Berne
AUSTRIA-HUNGARY
ROMANIA
Bucharest
BOSNIA
SERBIA
BULGARIA
BLACK SEA
MONTENEGRO
Sofia
ITALY
Constantinople
PORTUGAL
Madrid
Corsica
Rome
ALBANIA
OTTOMAN EMPIRE
(TURKEY)
Lisbon
SPAIN
Sardinia
GREECE
ATLANTIC
OCEAN
MEDITERRANEAN
Sicily
Athens
SEA
Cyprus

0   500 miles
0   500 kilometres

Otto von Bismarck, the first chancellor of Germany, negotiated an alliance with Austria-Hungary in 1879 (the Dual Alliance), and in 1882 with Austria-Hungary and Italy (the Triple Alliance). These agreements were based on defense—the countries promised to come to each other's aid if they were attacked. Prompted by fear of the power of the Triple Alliance, Russia and France made their own defensive alliance in 1894. Germany now had powerful potential enemies on both sides.

Britain remained aloof throughout the 19th century, secure in the prosperity gained from its industrial might and its vast empire. But by the beginning of the 20th century, the situation was beginning to look rather different. Other countries, including Germany, were starting to rival Britain's industrial output. The difficulties and high death toll of the Boer Wars (1899–1902) in South Africa also weakened Britain's once unshakeable confidence. In 1904, Britain entered into an agreement with France known as the Entente Cordiale. This was not a defensive agreement, as it dealt mainly with colonial matters, but it was nevertheless viewed as a military threat by Germany. A similar agreement was made with Russia in 1907, and soon people began to use the term "Triple Entente" to describe the alliance between Britain, France, and Russia.

? EVENT IN QUESTION

Did the alliance system help to start the war?

At first, defensive agreements were intended to reduce the possibility of one country declaring war on another from the opposing alliance. But some historians have argued that the alliances helped to turn a small, local quarrel into a major conflict. It is probably true that the alliances helped to provoke mistrust between the opposing European powers, and Germany certainly made war plans as a direct result of the perceived threat of the 1894 Franco-Russian agreement (see above). However, when matters came to a head in 1914, countries acted in their own national interests, often despite the terms of the alliances. For example, Italy refused to back its partners in the Triple Alliance, and Britain went to war in support of France even though it was not obliged to under the terms of the Triple Entente.

THE RACE TO ARMS

Throughout the 19th century, Britain had taken for granted the superiority of its navy over that of any other country. Then, in 1897, Admiral Alfred von Tirpitz, German State Secretary for the Navy, decided to begin building a German fleet to rival the British fleet. Tirpitz's goal was to construct a navy so powerful that it would threaten Britain's dominance of the seas and act as a deterrent to any confrontation. However, the British responded by increasing the rate of production of ships for their own fleet and in 1906 introduced the Dreadnought, a new type of battleship. Despite the costs of this naval arms race, Britain refused to give up its naval dominance because it considered the threat from Germany to be too great. When war broke out in 1914, Germany had 17 large warships, and Britain had 29.

Hand-in-hand with the building of battleships went the construction of new docks, and in Germany the widening of the Kiel Canal to allow even the largest battleships to sail between the Baltic Sea and the North Sea. There was also an acceleration in the production of other armaments. The Industrial Revolution, which started in Britain in the late 18th century, had a major impact on the manufacture of arms. Instead of being made individually by hand, from the 1840s onward, guns and other weapons could be mass-produced in factories. Business boomed for companies such as Krupps in Germany and Vickers in Britain —by 1914, the Krupps factories in Essen were Germany's biggest industrial works.

BELOW *The might of the British navy on display.*

Expanding the Military

Most European countries also built up large armed forces in readiness for a potential war. The exception was Britain, which had no history of mandatory military service. In Germany, the armed forces commanded huge respect, and the peacetime army was made up of 700,000 trained soldiers. The German commanders knew that if and when they decided to mobilize, they could also call on thousands more reservists to be ready within a week.

ABOVE *The armaments business: women fill shells with shrapnel at the Krupps factory in Essen, Germany.*

? EVENT IN QUESTION

Did the arms race contribute to the outbreak of war?

The naval arms race caused a great deal of antagonism between Germany and Britain. Propaganda reports in the press helped to stir up suspicion, setting the stage for a possible conflict. Sir Edward Grey, British Foreign Secretary, wrote in 1925, "The enormous growth of armaments in Europe, the sense of insecurity and fear caused by them—it was these that made the war inevitable. . . ." Many historians have questioned whether he was correct in his view. Although Britain spent the most on armaments in the pre-war years, it wanted war least. Germany spent less on defense than Britain, and yet it was deeply concerned about threats from Russia and France. It seems that the arms race was only one of many connected factors that pushed Europe from a fragile peace into all-out war.

TIPPING THE BALANCE

The event that tipped the scales toward war took place in Sarajevo in June 1914. Sarajevo was the capital of Bosnia-Herzegovina, a Balkan state that had been under the administration of Austria-Hungary since 1878 and was annexed (taken over) by Austria-Hungary in 1908. The population of Bosnia-Herzegovina included Serbs of Slavic origin who were deeply opposed to Austria-Hungary's rule. They were supported by many people in neighboring Serbia who believed that there should be a separate Slav state in the Balkans. Austria-Hungary wanted to increase its influence in the Balkans and regarded Serbia as a serious nuisance. Russia also supported its southern Slavic relations and had been prepared to mobilize troops in support of Serbia in the Balkan War of 1912–13. It was against this background of political turmoil that Archduke Franz Ferdinand, heir to the throne of Austria-Hungary, decided to visit Sarajevo in 1914.

Austrian diplomats advised the archduke not to make the visit, especially as the date on which it was to occur was Vivdovan,

BELOW *Archduke Franz Ferdinand and his wife Sophie with their entourage in Sarajevo on June 28, 1914. The events of this day ignited World War I.*

the most important Serbian national festival of the year. But the Archduke refused to listen to the warnings, and on June 28, he and his wife Sophie arrived in Sarajevo. The couple were driven around the streets of the city in an open-topped car. At one point a bomb was thrown at the car, but it bounced off and exploded behind the royal couple, leaving them unhurt. Then their car took a wrong turn, and as it slowed, shots rang out. Both the archduke and his wife were killed by Gavrilo Princip, a member of a Bosnian Serb nationalist group called the Black Hand Gang.

In Austria-Hungary, the news was greeted with outrage. The government decided to use the killings as an excuse to end Serbian influence in the Balkans, blaming the Serbian govern-ment for the assassination. Austria-Hungary knew it could rely on Germany's backing in the event of a war with Serbia; it also knew that going to war with Serbia might provoke Russian inter-vention and therefore provoke a Europe-wide war. Nevertheless, on July 23, Austria-Hungary issued an ultimatum to Serbia that was made up of 10 demands designed to curb Serb nationalists. On Russia's advice, Serbia agreed to all of the demands except one, but Austria-Hungary refused to agree to anything but com-plete acceptance of the ultimatum. Five days later, on July 28, Austria-Hungary declared war on Serbia.

? WHAT IF...

Archduke Franz Ferdinand had listened to the advice not to visit Sarajevo?

We have seen that the conditions for war were already present in Europe in 1914. Two opposing alliances, the arms race, and the build-up of military power all led to a climate of fear and suspicion. Some historians think that both Austria-Hungary and Germany were looking for an excuse for war: Austria-Hungary wanted to settle its claims in the Balkans, and Germany was feeling increasingly under threat from its powerful neighbors France and Russia. However, most people assumed that any war that did break out would be a short one. The death of the archduke provided the spark that lit the fuse of war, but it is likely that if he had visited Sarajevo on another day and survived, another excuse to start a conflict would have cropped up somewhere else.

ABOVE *War is declared in Germany: the official announcement is read to a packed crowd.*

DECLARING WAR

It is possible that the decision-makers in the government of Austria-Hungary thought they would be able to make a quick strike on Serbia and achieve their objectives before Russia could act. But they were wrong. Russia mobilized its army on July 30, two days after Austria-Hungary's declaration of war, although it still expressed a strong desire for a negotiated settlement. In response, Germany issued an ultimatum to Russia to stop its military preparations, and when Russia refused, Germany declared war on Russia on August 1. This brought the German Schlieffen Plan (see page 12) into immediate action, and the next day, Germany asked Belgium for safe passage for its troops on their way to attack France. Belgium refused, Germany declared war on France on August 3, and German troops invaded Belgium the following day.

Up until this point, Britain had remained on the sidelines, although Sir Edward Grey had made efforts to solve the crisis through diplomacy. The British government refused to give a direct commitment to support France if it was attacked by Germany, but it was the issue of Belgian neutrality that eventually drew Britain into the conflict. Since 1839, there had been an international agreement to respect Belgian neutrality, so when Germany violated this agreement, Britain was obliged to respond. Britain declared war on Germany on August 4, and the first British troops were sent to France soon after.

THE AMERICAN RESPONSE

Across the Atlantic Ocean, people in the United States greeted the news of war in Europe with shock, but few thought that America would become involved. In 1914, America took a neutral stance, favoring neither the Allies (France, Russia, and Britain) nor the Central Powers (Germany and Austria-Hungary). In theory, American companies were free to export arms and supplies to countries on either side of the conflict. However, Britain used its superior naval forces to blockade the Central Powers and keep supplies from getting through. This meant that American trade with Germany declined while trade with Britain and France increased. In 1915, Germany responded to the blockade by using its fleet of submarines (called U-boats) to blockade British waters. Disaster struck when a German U-boat attacked and sank a British passenger ship, the *Lusitania*, on May 7, 1915. More than 1,000 people drowned, including 128 American citizens. The incident provoked outrage in the U.S. and marked a turning point in American attitudes. However, it was another two years before the U.S. entered the war (see page 29).

? WHAT IF...

Britain had stayed out of the war?

If Britain had not declared war on August 4, 1914, British troops would not have gone to France two days later. It seems most likely that Germany would have overcome French resistance. There would have been no Battle of the Marne (see page 14) and no Western Front. The war may not have become a world war, nor would the United States have become involved. In his book *The Pity of War*, historian Niall Ferguson suggests that a rapid German victory would have eventually resulted in the transformation of Europe into something like "the European Union we know today . . ." but without the two world wars of the 20th century. He goes on to call World War I the "greatest error of modern history."

CHAPTER 2

Scenes of Battle

THE SCHLIEFFEN PLAN

When France and Russia entered into a formal alliance in 1894, Germany's response was to draw up a military plan for possible future war. The "Schlieffen Plan" was named after the German Chief of General Staff, Alfred von Schlieffen.

The Schlieffen Plan aimed to avoid fighting a war on two fronts at the same time: a rapid victory against France in the west was planned before moving east to crush Russia. The border between Germany and France was heavily fortified on the French side, so Schlieffen decided the attack on France would take place further west, by sending the right wing of a huge army through Belgium and then turning westward to Paris. A left wing would attack France through Alsace-Lorraine. The planned outcome was that the French army would be trapped between the two wings. The plan depended upon railroads to move troops and equipment efficiently to the German border. It also depended upon speed.

RIGHT *The Schlieffen Plan.*

Schlieffen retired in 1906, and his place was taken by Helmuth von Moltke, who eventually put the plan into action. The demands of the Schlieffen Plan meant that as soon as Russia started to mobilize its troops in July 1914, Germany had to move quickly against France. German troops invaded Belgium on August 4; by August 20, they had captured Brussels. They encountered more resistance than expected from the Belgians, but it was not enough to hold them back. Meanwhile, the British Expeditionary Force (BEF) (see page 14) had landed in northern France and made its way toward the fighting. The first battle to involve the BEF was at Mons, and although it halted the Germans for several days, it was indecisive. The French army and the BEF began to retreat southward. However, on August 26, Moltke diverted many troops from the right wing in Belgium to East Prussia, where there was trouble with the Russians. The Germans now lacked sufficient troops to encircle Paris, and the Schlieffen Plan began to unravel.

? EVENT IN QUESTION

What was wrong with Schlieffen's plan?

Even before war was declared, there were concerns about the Schlieffen Plan. Could sufficient German troops move rapidly enough to overwhelm the French forces without becoming exhausted or running out of supplies? Would Russia mobilize more quickly than the Germans thought they could? When Moltke took over from Schlieffen, he increased the size of the German army but was unable to resolve the problems of movement and supply. German troops often marched until they were exhausted, frequently going without food because supplies could not keep up. The plan also started to fail as it was adapted on the ground. Moltke weakened the right wing by removing troops to go to East Prussia, and German general Alexander von Kluck moved the army under his command southeast toward Paris, rather than in the westward pincer movement outlined in the Schlieffen Plan.

THE ALLIES ATTACK

Although the Schlieffen Plan was proving unworkable, German troops were within 30 miles (48 km) of Paris by the beginning of September 1914. The city emptied as residents fled, and the French government moved to Bordeaux. Moving in the opposite direction, French reservists hurried to the front line traveling by any means possible—including 600 taxis commandeered by the military. Moltke sensed victory, but the German troops had marched continuously for 33 days, and the men were exhausted. When the French and British began to attack along the River Marne, the Germans were unable to resist. The Battle of the Marne was inconclusive, but it prevented the Germans from marching into Paris. On September 9, Moltke ordered the German armies to retreat to safer defensive positions north of the Marne. The Schlieffen Plan was finally at an end.

The German armies retreated to the River Aisne, where they began preparing defensive fortifications on high ground north of the river—the first trenches of the war. Moltke had failed, and he was replaced by General Erich von Falkenhayn.

THE RACE TO THE SEA

The Allies attempted several attacks on the Aisne but found the German positions too strong. What followed was a series of attacks to the north of the Aisne, as both sides tried to establish superiority in the area of land between the Aisne and the sea. This is often referred to as the "Race to the Sea," as the Germans tried to keep the BEF from the Channel ports and a means of retreat. The culmination of these maneuvers was the First Battle of Ypres in October 1914, when the British force, with vital reinforcements from Indian units, managed to hold the line. It was at a great cost, however. The original BEF was almost wiped out, and thousands of young German student volunteers died in the fighting.

STALEMATE

As the First Battle of Ypres drew to a close and winter started to set in, neither side was in a position to launch a new offensive. Both the Germans and the Allies dug themselves into defensive trenches that now stretched in a line more than 338 miles (540 km) long, from the North Sea to Switzerland. In four months, the war had gone from one of rapid movement to complete stalemate. Both sides were exhausted, short of ammunition, and shocked by the already huge losses. It was the beginning of the war of attrition.

ABOVE *The British Expeditionary Force (BEF) in Ypres in October 1914. By the end of the war, the town of Ypres was completely devastated.*

? WHAT IF...

The Germans had captured Paris?

If the Germans had been able to continue the momentum of their great march southward another 30 miles (48 km) to Paris, the story of World War I would have been very different. There would have been no "Race to the Sea" and no First Battle of Ypres. In all probability, the BEF would have returned home largely unscathed. The Germans would have taken control of the channel ports, straining relations with Britain, but it is likely that Britain's involvement in the war would have been at an end. Parts of France would have been taken over by Germany, fueling even more antagonism between the two countries. But with no Western Front, millions of lives would have been spared.

ATTACK OR DEFEND?

In August 1914, it was Germany who had attacked, across Belgium and into northern France. But as stalemate set in after the First Battle of Ypres, the Germans adopted a different strategy. Instructed by Moltke in September 1914 to "entrench and hold" the positions reached after the Battle of the Marne, they constructed deep, strongly fortified trench systems that became increasingly sophisticated as the war progressed. The Germans hoped to keep things relatively quiet on the Western Front because of their need to move troops to the east, where, in January 1915, reinforcements were needed to fight the Russians.

The Allies, meanwhile, were more interested in a strategy of attack. For the French it was a matter of national economics and pride. The areas captured by the Germans were largely industrial regions of France, and it was unthinkable to the French commander, Marshal Joseph Joffre, that his troops should spend time

BELOW *The Western Front.*

16

and effort building a strong defensive line. His policy was to be one of attack and recovery of the captured land.

The British command put its faith in an ability to wear the enemy down by inflicting more casualties on the Germans than the Germans could inflict on the Allies—a war of attrition.

On March 16, 1917, the Germans once again used defensive tactics to strengthen their position on the Western Front. They began Operation Alberich to withdraw from certain sections of the Western Front to a previously prepared and heavily fortified defensive line about 19 miles (30 km) behind their old positions. The withdrawal shortened the German front line, making it easier to defend, and freed up more troops to be sent to the east. The new line was known to the Germans as the Siegfried Line, and to the Allies as the Hindenburg Line after the German commander, Field Marshal Paul von Hindenburg.

BELOW *German troops in a trench in 1914. Many German trenches were deep and well-constructed, as shown here.*

? EVENT IN QUESTION

What were the benefits of the different trench systems?

As the war continued, the Germans refined their tactics of defense. Along the Hindenburg Line, a system of defensive lines up to 4.5 miles (7.3 km) deep was created so that attacking troops would become exhausted before they could penetrate beyond the final line of defense. Another innovation was to dig front lines on the far side of hills, rather than on the slope facing the enemy. This meant that troops were hidden from the opposing enemy lines. Lookouts and machine-gunners would sound the alarm if enemies approached, and enemies would be attacked as they came over the crest of the hill.

VERDUN 1916

By the end of 1915, French casualties numbered more than 200,000, half of them dead. The German commander General Erich von Falkenhayn decided to launch an offensive early in 1916 to lure the French army into combat and inflict more damage on the French forces. He chose the area of the front line around the fortress of Verdun as the site for his offensive. Falkenhayn guessed that French pride would not allow Verdun to be given up easily, and he calculated that for every German killed in the attack, three French soldiers would die.

What Falkenhayn did not know was that, despite its formidable fortifications, Verdun and its surrounding forts had mostly been stripped of guns and troops. The French had watched the ease with which the Belgian fortresses of Liège and Namur had

BELOW *A deserted trench surrounded by deep mud and corpses at Fort Douaumont during the Battle of Verdun.*

fallen to the Germans in 1914 and had decided that such fortifications were ineffective against heavy German guns. So when operation Gericht ("judgment") was launched in February, the French were largely unprepared. The Germans quickly made progress, capturing the major stronghold of Fort Douaumont. Falkenhayn began to worry that Verdun would fall too easily without the war of attrition he had planned. But as the situation became critical, the French command decided that Verdun was to be defended as a matter of honor—just as Falkenhayn had hoped.

General Henri Pétain was put in charge of French operations at Verdun, and soon reinforcements were arriving along the only supply route into the fort on the French side, known as *la voie sacrée* ("the sacred way"). The fighting dragged on for months as the two sides attacked and counterattacked. Both the Germans and the French sustained heavy casualties, proving Falkenhayn's gruesome calculation wrong. In the beginning of May, General Robert Nivelle took over command of the French troops from Pétain. After a particularly intensive German barrage in June, he strengthened the resolve of his troops with the words, "On ne passe pas!" ("They shall not pass!").

The turning point of the battle for Verdun came in June. Just as in 1914, the German high command was forced to withdraw some troops from the Western Front at Verdun to send to the east, where the Russians had launched a new offensive. Soon after, the British forces attacked on the Somme (see page 21). By fall, the French began to regain territory, making use of new tactics such as the creeping barrage (see page 37), introduced by Nivelle. But it was not until August 1917 that the French recovered their front line positions of February 1916.

> **? WHAT IF...**
>
> ### The French had decided not to defend Verdun?
>
> Despite a reputation as a tenacious defender, Pétain had his doubts about the wisdom of defending Verdun. In March 1917, he suggested to the French president, Raymond Poincaré, the possibility of withdrawing from the fort and allowing the Germans to take it. The answer came back: "Don't think of it, General. It would be a parliamentary catastrophe." And so the fate of one and a half million soldiers was sealed. If the French had chosen not to defend, or if the Germans had been able to press their advantage and take the fort, it is possible that the war would have ended far sooner, as France may have accepted some kind of compromise agreement with Germany.

THE SOMME, 1916

Early in 1916, the Allies began to plan a joint attack against the German front line in the area of the Somme. The new British commander, Douglas Haig, would have preferred to mount an offensive around Ypres but conceded to the insistence of French commander Marshal Joseph Joffre to attack where British and French forces met. Haig hoped to make a breakthrough on the Somme and push the Germans back. Joffre's aim was one of attrition—to kill as many Germans as possible.

The timing of the Somme attack was affected by German advances at Verdun (see pages 18–19). Joffre and Pétain appealed to Haig for the Somme offensive to start as soon as possible to relieve their forces. Haig reluctantly agreed that the attack should start several weeks earlier than originally planned, on July 1, 1916, and that British troops would play the major role. Many of these troops were volunteers, part of "Kitchener's Army" (see page 30). They were joined by forces from Australia, Canada, India, New Zealand, and South Africa.

? PEOPLE IN QUESTION

General Sir Douglas Haig (1861–1928)

In accounts of the Battle of the Somme, Haig was greatly criticized. He was suspicious of officers below him and unwilling to listen to advice. He was convinced that only a major attack on the Western Front would finally bring the war to an end. So when British patrols brought news that the preliminary bombardment had had little effect on the German wire or front lines, Haig's second-in-command failed to pass this information on—he knew Haig did not respond well to criticism. On June 30, Haig noted in his diary that the wire "had never been so well cut, nor the artillery preparation so thorough. . . ."

Many soldiers in Kitchener's volunteer army were only half-trained, and few had any experience in battle. Haig ordered a massive artillery bombardment of the German front line starting on June 24. His hope was that the shelling would empty the German front lines and rip holes in the barbed wire in No Man's Land (see page 32). In fact, the Germans had built deep protective dugouts in the Somme and retreated there during the shelling, which also proved ineffective against the wire.

On July 1, the Allied attack began. The plan was that waves of Allied troops would proceed out of their front lines, through the gaps created in the German barbed wire, and into the empty German front lines. However, the Germans set up their machine guns and shot down the attacking troops. It was the worst day in British military history: the troops suffered about 60,000 casualties, 20,000 of whom died. Yet the battle continued until November 19. Allied casualties amounted to 600,000 men, and they gained about seven miles (11 km) of territory.

ABOVE *A wounded British soldier is carried to safety during one of the battles of the Somme offensive in 1916. Heavy fall rains had turned the battlefield into a sea of deep, stinking mud.*

Robert Nivelle (1857–1924)

How did Nivelle manage to convince people that his attack should go ahead, and what made him so sure that it would be successful? Nivelle was charming, handsome, and very confident. He spoke perfect English and quickly won over the British Prime Minister, David Lloyd George, who preferred to trust the French general rather than Douglas Haig. When Nivelle's plan was met with resistance in his own government, he threatened to resign, which quickly silenced all opposition. Fresh off the recapture of Verdun, Nivelle was eager to use the same tactics again. However, Nivelle did not consider the fact that his troops would be attacking a well-prepared and strongly held defensive line, and Nivelle's attack was a failure.

THE NIVELLE OFFENSIVE

In December 1916, after the failure of the Somme campaign and the fighting at Verdun, French general Robert Nivelle replaced Joffre as commander of the French troops on the Western Front. Nivelle had been responsible for the French recapture of Verdun, and he now wanted to build on this success. In January 1917, he explained his plans for a new attack to the British government.

The British commander, General Sir Douglas Haig, had planned to continue attacking the German front line on the Somme in 1917, but Nivelle wanted to concentrate a powerful attack in the Champagne region, to the east of the Somme, as well as a diversionary attack to the west of the Somme, around Arras. Nivelle declared: "We shall break the German front when we wish, provided we do not attack the strongest point and that we execute the operation by surprise and abrupt attack, in 24 hours or 48 hours." Nivelle's plan was that the two attacks should "squeeze" the westward bulge (known as a salient) in the German front line and eliminate it.

In fact, it did not require any fighting to eliminate the salient because, in March 1917, the Germans themselves withdrew to the formidable defenses of the Hindenburg Line (see page 17), destroying everything in their path as they retreated. Nevertheless, Nivelle was determined to continue with his planned offensive. Despite opposition to his plans in the French government, Nivelle finally convinced enough people that his offensive would bring about the end of the fighting on the Western Front.

The Battle of Arras started on April 9 and at first appeared to be a success as Canadian troops stormed onto Vimy Ridge. But the Allied commanders failed to take advantage of their troops' initial success, and by the time orders came for the attack, the Germans had had time to regroup. The French attacked in the Champagne region on April 16, along a part of the front line known as the "Chemin des Dames." But the Germans had plenty of warning of this attack and had been digging fortifications in this part of the line for more than two years. The attack continued for weeks but eventually failed. The French suffered more than 100,000 casualties, and mutinies broke out in the army (see page 53). On May 15, Nivelle was replaced as commander of the French forces by General Henri Pétain.

BELOW *French army cooks prepare food for the troops in the area of the front line known as the Chemin des Dames.*

THIRD YPRES / PASSCHENDAELE, 1917

In 1917, Haig finally succeeded in his desire to launch an attack in the area around Ypres. The French army was still recovering from the mutinies that had followed the Nivelle Offensive, so the initiative passed to the British. Haig's goal was to break through the German defenses at Ypres and retake Belgium, capturing the seaports of Zeebrugge and Ostende, from where it was believed German U-boats were operating. Prime Minister David Lloyd George was at first unwilling to allow the attack—he feared a repeat of the terrible slaughter of the Somme. But he was finally convinced by Haig and his advisers.

Haig's belief in the soundness of his plan was boosted by the capture of Messines Ridge in June 1917. This ridge formed the southern part of the Ypres salient, and it was vital that it be taken before the attack on Ypres could start. The British dug five miles (8 km) of tunnels beneath the ridge and packed them with explosives. When the explosives were detonated on June 7, the blast was heard in London. However, the capture of the ridge was followed by a seven-week lull as the British prepared for the major offensive. Once again, the British were attacking deep, well-prepared German defenses. Once again, as at the Somme, Haig planned a massive preliminary bombardment to pulverize the German defenses. The bombardment started on July 17 and lasted 14 days; more than four million shells were fired.

By the time of the first attack on July 31, another factor had come into play. The region is known for its unstable summer weather, and the summer of 1917 was particularly rainy. The ground, torn by shells, soon turned into thick mud so deep that men and horses drowned in it. The conditions were so bad that Haig suspended the attack on August 4, but he was still undeterred. The Third Battle of Ypres continued until November 18, ending with assaults on the ridge and what was left of the village of Passchendaele. The name Passchendaele came to refer to the whole offensive, and to many symbolized the futility of the war on the Western Front. There were more than 240,000 British casualties, thousands of whom simply disappeared into the mud.

? EVENT IN QUESTION

What effect did Passchendaele have on the British army?

In his book *The First World War*, the eminent military historian John Keegan wrote: "On the Somme he [Haig] had sent the flower of British youth to death or mutilation; at Passchendaele he had tipped the survivors into the slough of despond [the depths of despair]." Haig's reasoning for continuing the battle at Ypres is difficult to comprehend; the huge casualties left the British army with no reserves, and those who did survive had any remaining optimism crushed out of them by their experiences. In a letter, one soldier described ". . . the mile after mile of the same unending dreariness . . . whole villages hardly a pile of bricks amongst the mud . . ." and "the horror of continual shell fire, rain and mud. . . ." After the fighting had ended, Haig's chief of staff was taken to visit Passchendaele. It is said that he looked around in disbelief and exclaimed: "My God, did we really send men to fight in this?"

LUDENDORFF'S OFFENSIVE

In March 1918, the Russians signed the Treaty of Brest-Litovsk, and the war on the Eastern Front came to an end. This immediately freed German troops and guns to fight on the Western Front. There was a sense of urgency among the German high command because, in April 1917, the U.S. had entered the war, and the Germans knew that American troops would soon be joining the Allied forces. The commander of the German army, General Erich von Ludendorff, decided to attack the Allied armies in the spring of 1918 along the Somme. The attacks were designed to push the British army back toward the English Channel and the French army toward Paris, creating a gap between the two Allies. Then Ludendorff planned to crush the British forces, with the expectation that France would give up the fight without its ally.

The first attack, code-named Michael, began on March 21 with a bombardment of artillery, smoke and gas shells, machine-gun fire, and attacks from the air. By April 5, the Germans had

BELOW *The bodies of German troops are identified at a makeshift cemetery near the French town of Reims during the Ludendorff Offensive in 1918.*

advanced 20 miles (32 km) along a front of 50 miles (80 km) and created a 10-mile (16 km) gap in the Allied line. However, German casualties were high, and they were advancing across open land that they themselves had devastated during the withdrawal to the Hindenburg Line. Another hazard came in the form of the abandoned supplies of food and drink found by the German invaders, which often proved too tempting. One German officer complained, "entire divisions totally gorged themselves on food and liquor and failed to press the vital attack forward. . . ."

The apparent success of Operation Michael frightened the Allies, and, for the first time, the British and French agreed to unite under the leadership of Field-Marshal Ferdinand Foch, the French Chief of Staff. When the Germans attacked again on April 9 around Ypres, Haig issued the following order: "There is no course open to us but to fight it out. Every position must be held to the last man: there must be no retirement. With our backs to the wall and believing in the justice of our cause, we must fight on to the end. . . ."

Ludendorff launched more massive attacks along the Aisne and then, in July, in the Marne region. But American troops were now arriving by the thousands on the front line. Ludendorff's offensive had achieved massive territorial gains for the Germans, but at a great cost.

? EVENT IN QUESTION

Did Ludendorff's offensive strengthen or weaken the German position?

The territory the Germans gained in a few months as a result of Ludendorff's offensive came at a great human cost—hundreds of thousands of casualties. The only possible replacements for these men were convalescents and boys just turning 18. But the territorial gains meant that the German front line was longer and more vulnerable than before, and therefore needed more men to hold it. Meanwhile, thousands of American soldiers were arriving on the Allied front lines. Ludendorff's offensive may have frightened the Allies and inflicted serious damage on their forces, but it left Germany in a weaker position and caused the German troops to become increasingly demoralized.

THE ARRIVAL OF THE AMERICANS

When war broke out in 1914, the U.S. declared itself neutral. So why, three years later, did the Americans go to war on the side of the Allies? The British blockade of the Central Powers (see page 11) forced the Germans to resort to unrestricted submarine warfare—attacking merchant vessels without warning. This led to the sinking of the *Lusitania* in 1915 (see page 11) and the Germans renouncing the policy of attack without warning. But by the beginning of 1917, the situation in Germany was becoming so desperate that the German high command decided to start unrestricted submarine warfare once again. They knew that this move would bring the U.S. into the war, but they gambled that the Americans would not be able to mobilize fast enough to make a crucial difference.

BELOW *The arrival of American troops in Britain is greeted with great enthusiasm in August 1917. The troops were destined to fight on the Western Front in France.*

In January 1917, German foreign minister Arthur Zimmermann sent a telegram to the German ambassador in Mexico outlining a plan for Mexico to join the war on Germany's side if the U.S. entered the war. He also asked for Mexican help to persuade Japan to join the Central Powers against the Allies. He hoped that the U.S. would end up fighting a war on two fronts against Mexico and Japan, limiting its help to the Allies on the Western Front. The Zimmermann telegram was intercepted by the British, and its contents were sent to the American government.

ABOVE *American troops eating in a trench at Ancervilles in France in March 1918.*

The U.S. president, Woodrow Wilson, declared war on Germany on April 6, 1917, and appointed General John G. Pershing to command the American Expeditionary Force. The first American troops—nicknamed "doughboys"—began to arrive in France in late 1917, and the first battle involving American forces was at Cantigny in May 1918. Many American divisions fought under British or French command on the Western Front, but in September 1918, the U.S. army went into action as an independent unit at St. Mihiel. In the same month, American troops joined the French to push the Germans back in the Meuse-Argonne region.

? EVENT IN QUESTION

What role did the U.S. play in bringing the war to an end?

According to historian Allan Millett, "Although there was little doubt in the minds of the soldiers of the AEF—from General Pershing to the lowliest doughboy—that the Americans had won the war on the Western Front, a more accurate assessment is that the Allies might have lost the war without the American Expeditionary Forces." When the American soldiers arrived in France, many were only half-trained, and all were inexperienced. General Pershing was determined to wait until his troops were trained and ready to form independent units. But he was persuaded to allow American soldiers to serve under British and French commanders as a temporary measure. The influx of fresh troops, however inexperienced, immediately tipped the scales against Germany. It was clear that the American army would become stronger as 1919 approached, helping to convince the Germans that they were defeated on the Western Front.

Fighting the War

THE BRITISH ARMY

When war broke out in 1914, Britain had a small, professional army of about 240,000 regulars, half of whom formed the British Expeditionary Force (BEF) and half of whom were overseas. There was no mandatory military service, but there were reservists and Territorials who could be called upon in times of war. The regular soldiers were well-trained, and many had gained battle experience in South Africa in the Boer Wars. However, by the end of the First Battle of Ypres (see page 14), most of the original BEF was wiped out.

The drive for new recruits was led by the Secretary of State for War, Field Marshal Horatio Kitchener, who announced to a startled British government in August 1914 that he expected the war to last for three or four years and that a million men would be needed for the war effort. The government refused to introduce a military draft, so Kitchener relied on volunteers. He began a massive recruitment campaign, and the results were overwhelming. In all, more than three million men volunteered to serve in Kitchener's "new armies." However, the British army did not have

BELOW *British volunteers are fitted for army uniforms. By the end of 1914, a million men had joined Kitchener's "new armies."*

the manpower to sufficiently equip and train all these civilian volunteers, and many were sent to the Western Front ill-prepared for what awaited them. For many, their first taste of battle was at the Somme in July 1916 (see page 20). The British government finally introduced a draft in February 1916.

FRANCE AND GERMANY

Both the French and the Germans had bigger regular armies than the British in 1914, since both countries featured mandatory military service. France had an army of about 770,000 troops and 46,000 soldiers overseas. Germany's army was made up of about 700,000 men, and there were large numbers of reservists who could be called upon as soon as the army was mobilized for war.

ABOVE *German reservists say good-bye to their families before leaving Berlin for the front in 1914.*

U.S. FORCES

The U.S. joined the war in 1917, and the American government set up a draft system to bulk up the army. The American Expeditionary Force (AEF) was commanded by General John G. Pershing, who, having watched the slaughter on the Western Front from across the Atlantic, was unwilling to turn his troops over to the Allied commanders. Technically, the AEF remained a separate fighting force in France, although American troops did fight under British and French commanders (see page 29). Unwearied by the long years of the war of attrition that the Allied troops had suffered, the AEF brought much-needed reinforcement to the Allied front line. About two million American troops served in France; more than 50,000 died in combat.

? EVENT IN QUESTION

Why did so many British men volunteer for service?

The outbreak of war was greeted with a mixture of emotions. Sir Edward Grey made the comment that the war marked "the lamps going out all over Europe." Yet there was a great deal of public enthusiasm for the war. When Kitchener launched his recruitment campaign, there was a rush to join up—of all the men who volunteered for Kitchener's armies, 29 percent joined up within the first eight weeks. The reasons for this rush included a sense of patriotism, a fear of a German invasion of Britain, a sense of adventure, and pressure from friends, wives, and sweethearts to "do your duty for your country."

TRENCH WARFARE

As the Allies and the Germans fought to a standstill in 1914, soldiers on both sides took refuge in pits and ditches, which they soon enlarged to form continuous trenches. This system of trenches eventually stretched more than 338 miles (540 km), from the North Sea to Switzerland.

NO MAN'S LAND

Between the front line trenches of the opposing sides lay a strip of land that became known as No Man's Land. Both sides positioned rolls of barbed wire in No Man's Land to protect their front lines. The width of No Man's Land varied greatly along the Western Front. On average, it was between 330 and 660 feet (100–200 m), but in some places it was as little as 60 feet (18 m) or as much as one mile (1.6 km). During the day, No Man's Land could be eerily silent and still, but at night there was often considerable activity as both sides sent out patrols to spy on the enemy's activities and wiring parties to improve defenses. Raiding was also an important part of trench warfare. Groups of raiders would creep through prepared holes in the wire to launch surprise attacks on the opposing front line. The goal was to kill as many enemy troops as possible, to take prisoners, and to gain intelligence.

BELOW *Soldiers line up in a trench before launching a raid into No Man's Land. The moment when a soldier left the (relative) safety of the trench to start an attack was known as "going over the top."*

TRENCH SYSTEMS

The trench systems of the British, French, and Germans varied slightly, but they all included a front line, from which attacks were launched, and various supporting trenches dug at intervals parallel to and behind the front line. The British developed a three-tier system of front, support, and reserve lines. The front line usually had two trenches, a firing trench and a command trench, connected by communications trenches. The support and reserve lines, behind the front line, were also connected by communications trenches. They allowed reinforcements to reach the front line troops. The artillery was set up behind the reserve lines.

The French system was slightly different, with front and support lines, while the Germans built highly sophisticated trench systems. Although diagrams of trench systems make them look organized and neat, the reality was often very different. As the war progressed and trenches were destroyed and re-dug, occupied and abandoned, in some places the front line became maze-like, and fresh troops often needed a guide to lead them to their positions.

BELOW *British soldiers eat part of their daily rations during the Somme offensive.*

? EVENT IN QUESTION

How did soldiers survive life on the Western Front?

One of the ways in which soldiers on both sides of the Western Front made life more bearable was by an unofficial and unspoken policy of "live and let live." At times, troops deliberately avoided or restricted aggressive activity in return for the same avoidance or restriction from the enemy. The most basic motive behind this arrangement was a desire to stay alive, rather than to "kill and be killed." It also allowed troops to perform the necessities of everyday life: eat hot food, sleep, and delouse themselves (lice were a constant presence in the trenches). "Live and let live" was strictly forbidden by the high command of both sides, who thought that front line troops should spend their time harassing the enemy. It was, nevertheless, a fact of life on many parts of the front throughout the war.

WEAPONS OF WAR

The main weapon for the infantry (foot soldiers) was the rifle. Every soldier had a rifle equipped with a bayonet, a sharp blade that was attached to the end of the rifle for use in close-range attacks. Troops in the front line had to always be on guard against snipers in the enemy lines. If an unwary soldier allowed his head to show above the top of the trench, he was likely to be killed by a bullet through the skull. Troops used periscopes to peer over the edge of the trench to see No Man's Land and the enemy front line beyond, but even the lens of a periscope was a target for a sharpshooter. Snipers' rifles could also be fixed on a position where it was known that lookout was kept, so that sniping could continue at night.

BELOW *German troops rifle training during the early days of the war.*

Troops were also issued grenades and bombs, but the other main front-line weapon was the machine gun. This weapon could fire continuous rounds of bullets loaded onto a belt—from 250 to 600 rounds a minute depending upon the type of gun. The gun was mounted on a tripod and was manned by a crew of 6 to 10 men. It could be set to fire on a fixed trajectory along the enemy's front line, so in the event of an attack the crew simply had to man

ABOVE *A German machine gun crew in a trench on the Western Front.*

the gun as fast as possible and start firing. The drawback of the machine gun was that it was heavy and difficult to move, and it needed a large crew to fire it—although there are tales of one solitary machine-gunner heroically operating his weapon alone as a last stand.

Behind the trenches were the big guns—the artillery—manned by teams of gunners. It was the artillery and their shells that caused most casualties along the Western Front. The artillery were used to preface attacks by firing planned bombardments, such as the one before the Third Battle of Ypres (see page 25). The big guns could also respond to new information from the front line, pinpointing an exact location for shelling the enemy. They also needed to react quickly to SOS calls—usually signal lights—if the front line was under attack.

? EVENT IN QUESTION

What were the pros and cons of a preliminary bombardment?

The Allied policy of using artillery gave notice to the Germans that an attack was going to happen in a particular place along the front line. And although day after day of heavy shelling undoubtedly had an effect on the morale of the Germans, because of the strength of the German defenses it usually did not force them to abandon their positions as the Allies intended. The impact of thousands of shells exploding on the ground created huge holes—not ideal for the attackers, who had to navigate their way through and around the craters. It also made it difficult for the artillery to be moved forward to provide cover for an advancing army. Nevertheless, the Allied high command remained unwilling to launch an attack without the precaution of a preliminary bombardment.

ABOVE *German nurses wear gas masks as they treat two victims of an Allied gas attack.*

New Tactics

Almost as soon as the trenches were dug, inventors began to devise new weapons and technologies for use on the Western Front. It soon became clear that fresh ideas were going to be needed to try to break the deadlock between the two sides. The British government was bombarded with ideas for new and improved weapons, only a very few of which were accepted for use in the trenches. One of these was the trench mortar, designed by F.W. Stokes. This weapon allowed bombs to be fired from the trenches, and by 1916, there were three different types, the largest of which could send a 150-pound (70 kg) bomb more than half a mile. Although trench mortars allowed a more rapid and accurate response to any enemy activity than an SOS call to the artillery, the infantry was wary of these weapons. They were so effective that they tended to provoke angry retaliation from the enemy. As one military historian recorded, "owing to the retaliation provoked by their use, those operating them [trench mortars] were very unpopular with the occupants of the various trenches. . . .”

Other new technologies that came into use were aircraft (see page 40), tanks (see page 42), and gas. The first use of gas on the Western Front was by the Germans on April 22, 1915, at Langemarck, north of Ypres, during the Second Battle of Ypres. The Germans released 5,000 cylinders of chlorine gas that drifted on the wind over the Allied trenches. Thousands of French troops fled as the gas choked them, and many died. Crude gas masks were quickly improvised to try to protect front line troops from similar attacks. However, the Allies were also developing their own poison gases, and they first used gas in an attack at Loos on September 15, 1915.

One notable tactical innovation introduced during the war on the Western Front was the “creeping barrage.” This tactic used the artillery to protect the infantry and to “neutralize” the enemy during an attack. It was introduced during 1916, and the principle was that a wall of shells should fall just ahead of the attacking troops. This wall moved forward by a few yards every few minutes, followed as fast as possible by the attacking soldiers. The goal was to keep the enemy pinned down in their trenches, unable to man their rifles and machine guns. It relied heavily on the accuracy of the artillery—who of course could not see what they were firing at (see page 38). Nevertheless, it became an important tactic in offensives along the Western Front.

? EVENT IN QUESTION

How effective was gas?

Both sides used various forms of gas: chlorine, the more lethal phosgene, and mustard gas, which burned and blistered the skin and often caused temporary blindness. Mustard gas was first used by the Germans in July 1917 to great effect. However, by 1916, both sides had introduced gas masks as standard issue, which gave the infantry some protection against these attacks. Gas attacks were difficult to manage, because once the canisters were opened, a change in the wind could easily blow the gas back onto the attacker's own front line. Throughout the war, gas tended to incapacitate more troops than it killed. Still, it was a useful weapon because it removed large numbers of troops from the front line while they recovered.

ABOVE *A German soldier uses a field telephone to send information during the fighting at Verdun.*

COMMUNICATIONS

In the age of radio, television, the Internet, and the mobile phone, it is difficult to grasp how basic the means of communication were during World War I. Relaying commands and information from one part of the battlefield to another, or from headquarters and back, was one of the biggest challenges faced by both sides on the Western Front. Wireless radio sets were being developed during the war, but they were very large and heavy, needing 12 men to transport all of the components.

The main form of communication from the front line back to headquarters and to other areas of the front line was by telephone. Wires were laid beneath the ground in places where they were less likely to be broken by shelling—experience showed that they needed to be at least six feet (1.8 m) below the surface to be completely safe. However, burying cable so deep was time-consuming work, and once the cable was in place, it could not be easily moved. The system worked reasonably well, though, until an attack was launched. As attacking soldiers moved forward toward the enemy, they were inevitably moving further away from the nearest point of communication. Troops unwound telephone cable as they attacked, but it was almost always broken during the fighting. Other methods of communication included signal lights, human runners, carrier pigeons, and even message-carrying dogs.

One vital area of communication was between the front line and the artillery. The gunners who manned the artillery usually fired without being able to see their targets—if they could see the enemy, they could also be seen and were therefore vulnerable. They relied on information from lookout posts along the front line, and later in the war from observation balloons and aircraft. The problem was that once the telephone lines were broken, messages traveled only as fast as a human runner, or if visibility was good enough, a flag signal could be used. To aim their guns, the artillery gunners used maps and aerial photographs taken from aircraft. Aircraft and scouts in balloons were also used to see if the shells were falling in the correct area during an attack.

ABOVE *A messenger dog used to carry food to German troops on the front line.*

? EVENT IN QUESTION

How big a part did the difficulties of communication on the front line play in the war of attrition?

Difficulties in communication meant that it was much easier for defenders, falling back to their reserve trenches, to make a coherent plan than for attackers to communicate with each other and with their commanders. As it was most often the Allies who were on the offensive, this became a particular problem for them. Commanders such as Sir Douglas Haig have often been accused of being out of touch with the reality of what was happening on the Western Front, and of failing to react quickly enough to events during battle. But it could take many hours for a message to travel from the front line back to headquarters—by which time the situation on the front could have changed completely. It was difficult, therefore, for plans to be adapted according to circumstances and probably partly explains why most attacks on the Western Front ended indecisively or in failure.

WAR IN THE AIR

Troops sheltering in the trenches of the Western Front were sometimes entertained by dogfights between German and Allied aircraft in the air above the front line. Often these fights ended in the crash of one or both planes and the inevitable death of the pilots. Pilots were not equipped with parachutes, and in 1917, the life expectancy of a new British pilot was between 11 days and 3 weeks. In 1914, the British Royal Flying Corps had just 63 machines—by 1918, the newly formed Royal Air Force had 22,000 aircraft.

The primary function of airplanes during World War I was reconaissance and observation—spotting artillery, shooting down enemy observation balloons, and similar tasks. Their work was vital to produce the maps and photos of the Western Front needed by the artillery gunners and to plan attacks. As the Germans had the advantage of the high ground along much of the Western Front, dominating the air became important for the Allies. However, the Germans responded by sending up their own planes to stop the Allies' aerial activities. This led to the development of fighting techniques in the air.

At first, pilots took small guns with them to shoot at their enemies. Then, in 1915, a French pilot named Roland Garros devised a method of attaching a machine gun to his plane. But a few weeks later, he crashed behind German lines, and his invention was adapted by Dutch engineer Anthony Fokker for the Germans. By 1916, both sides were using similar technology, and aerial combat led to the development of fast "fighter" planes such as the Sopwith Camel.

Pilots who survived for any length of time were acclaimed as heroes. These air "aces" included German Manfred von Richthofen, French pilot Georges Guynemer, and British pilots Albert Ball and Edward "Mick" Mannock, all of whom were shot down and killed. American pilots also flew on the Western Front before the U.S. entered the war as part of the "Escadrille Americaine" founded in 1916 and made up of American volunteers who were eager to see action in France.

By 1917, both sides started to use aircraft to attack troops on the ground and developed bombers for attacks on the Western Front and on the enemies' home fronts. The Germans used lighter-than-air dirigibles (air balloons) called Zeppelins to mount bombing raids on London from 1915 onward. They later used Gotha bombers for air raids, while the British developed the Handley-Page bomber.

ABOVE *Aerial combat in the skies above the Western Front: a British plane shoots down its German enemy.*

? PEOPLE IN QUESTION

Manfred von Richthofen (1882–1918)

German flying "ace" Manfred von Richthofen started the war in a cavalry regiment. In 1915, bored with the inactivity of the trenches, he joined the German air service and became very interested in aerial combat. He acquired the nickname the "Red Baron" because of the color of his Fokker plane and was credited with shooting down 80 enemy planes before his own death on April 21, 1918. There are two accounts of his death: that he was shot down by antiaircraft fire from the ground, or that he was shot down by Captain A. Roy Brown, a Canadian pilot serving in the Royal Air Force.

ABOVE *A Belgian armored car that would have been used at the beginning of the war. Later in the war, tanks replaced armored cars.*

THE ALLIED SECRET WEAPON

As early as the fall of 1914, the British government began to look into the possibility of building a vehicle that could cross trenches, break through barbed wire, and eliminate machine guns. In 1915, both the British and the French developed the first tanks, although they worked independently on these projects. The word "tank" came from the crates that the British used to transport these secret machines to France—they were originally called "land-ships," but this name soon died out. The French called their tanks "chars" (chariots).

The leading role in the development of tanks in Britain was taken by Colonel Ernest Swinton. He was very enthusiastic about the new invention and had specific ideas about how it should be used. He said that tanks should not appear on the battlefield until there were enough of them to make an impact and to take the enemy completely by surprise. He also thought that they should support the infantry in an attack, breaking a hole in the enemy line to allow the soldiers to pour through. He was ignored, however. General Douglas Haig was eager to make use of the few tanks that were ready by the summer of 1916, and so the Allies' secret weapon made its debut at the Somme on September 15, 1916.

It wasn't a complete success. Although the appearance of 36 tanks terrified the unsuspecting German troops, nearly all of the tanks broke down or became stuck in rough ground. Nevertheless, Haig was impressed enough with their performance to order 1,000 more tanks. However, it was not until November 1917 that tanks made the impact on the battlefield that Colonel Swinton had envisioned. At the Battle of Cambrai, the Allies used more than 350 tanks in a massed attack against the German front line. This was the first time that tanks formed a key part of the plan of attack, and it was initially very successful. After a short, intense artillery bombardment, the tanks led the attack, followed closely by the infantry. Most of the German troops simply fled, and by the end of the day, church bells rang out in Britain to signal an Allied victory. However, the Germans counterattacked, and by the end of the battle in early December, little ground was gained by either side.

? EVENT IN QUESTION

Were tanks a war-winning weapon?

The Germans built a few prototype tanks but then decided that tanks were too unreliable and concentrated their efforts on other technology. Indeed, British tanks were slow and too liable to break down to be truly effective. More reliable were the French Renault tanks, which were lighter and faster. Nevertheless, after the lessons learned at the Battle of Cambrai, tanks went on to play an important role in the battles of 1918. Tanks were most useful when used in combination with the artillery and infantry. They were not, however, a war-winning weapon in their own right, nor did they offer a solution to the stalemate on the Western Front.

BELOW *A tank being used on the Western Front. Tanks played an important part in the later battles of the war.*

REPORTING THE WAR

So much is known about World War I today, and information is so readily available, that it is difficult to believe how little information about the Western Front battles reached people at home during the war itself. As soon as war broke out, governments moved to censor the press. In Britain, the Defense of the Realm Act was passed on August 8, 1914. It forbade the publishing of any information that could be of use to the enemy, as well as news that could undermine loyalty to the king or affect recruitment. Similar laws were also passed in France and Germany. The problem for newspapers was that information of use to the enemy covered almost anything—from troop movements to weather reports.

At the beginning of the war, Lord Kitchener, Minister for War in Britain (see page 30), banned war correspondents from a set zone around the BEF in France. Instead, a Press Bureau was set up that received reports from the military, censored them, and then issued them to the press. As battles raged across Belgium and northern France, the gap between the reality of the war and the news bulletins began to widen. Some war correspondents decided to risk arrest, or worse, and set off across northern France to try to determine what was really happening.

The strict censorship of news caused a major problem for governments, however. On one hand, people at home were being urged to help the war effort by signing up for service, manufacturing weapons, and other war work. On the other hand, the seriousness of the situation in France was rarely portrayed in the newspapers. The government needed the support of the general public, and the press was very influential in forming the opinion of the public. Accordingly, in May 1915, five war correspondents were allowed to travel to and report on the Western Front. They wore uniforms and were accompanied at all times by an official censor. Their reports continued to downplay the negative aspects of the war and to recount stories of heroism and valor. The general public relied on rumors, on letters from their loved ones at the front (also censored), and on the accounts of those home on leave for news of the truth of the war.

? EVENT IN QUESTION

Why did the general public accept such huge casualty figures?

"If the people really knew, the war would be stopped tomorrow. But of course they don't—and can't know. The correspondents don't write and the censorship would not pass the truth." These words from British Prime Minister David Lloyd George offer a clue about the public acceptance of casualty figures. The public didn't know the truth, and the reality of battles such as those at the Somme or Passchendaele didn't become fully known until the 1920s. Dispatches sent on July 1, 1916, were vague but optimistic: "It is too early as yet to give anything but the barest particulars, as the fighting is developing in intensity, but the British troops have already occupied the German front line. Many prisoners have already fallen into our hands, and as far as can be ascertained our casualties have not been heavy." In fact, 20,000 British troops died on that day alone (see page 21).

Life on the Western Front

CHRISTMAS 1914

The winter of 1914 was wet, cold, and utterly miserable for the troops sheltering in the muddy trenches of the Western Front. But Christmas Day 1914 dawned cold and frosty, freezing the mud solid and coating everything with a dazzling white frost. The previous night there had been singing in the trenches, with "Silent Night" and "O Come All Ye Faithful" drifting across the cold air. As day dawned and the sun gradually burned away the early morning mist, the soldiers got out of the trenches and began to walk around, warming themselves up.

BELOW *German officers celebrate Christmas in the trenches.*

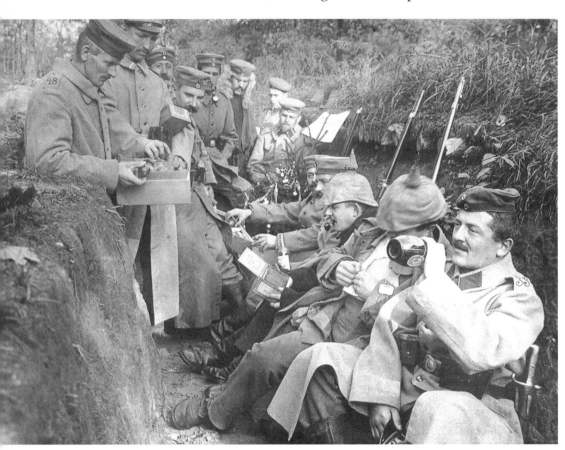

It soon became clear that the enemy soldiers were doing likewise, and it wasn't long before British and German soldiers, and French and German soldiers, were meeting in No Man's Land. The enemy soldiers exchanged Christmas greetings and gave each other small gifts of cigarettes, cigars, chocolates, and buttons. Some soldiers even went into the enemy trenches; others took group photos to commemorate the occasion. In some places, impromptu games of soccer were played. In others, troops took advantage of the truce to bury the bodies of dead comrades that lay in No Man's Land. Throughout the day, not a shot was fired.

One British soldier described the Christmas Day truce in a letter home to his family: "On that day [Christmas Day] everyone spontaneously left their trenches and had a meeting halfway between the trenches. Germans gave us cigars, and we gave them chocolate and tobacco. They seemed very pleased to see us!" In fact, the Christmas truces were part of the more prevalent "live and let live" system that was an element of everyday life in the trenches (see page 33). In many places, the Christmas truce went on for days, without any shots being fired from either side. As usual, this peace met with official disapproval, however, and orders came for the truce to stop. A British soldier wrote on December 30: "Same routine as before. Still no war! At about lunchtime however a message came down the line to say that [the] Germans had sent across to say that their General was coming along in the afternoon, so we had better keep down, as they might have to do a little shooting to make things look right!!! This we did, and a few shots came over about 3:30 P.M."

? EVENT IN QUESTION

Why did the Allied and German commanders ban any future fraternization?

When word of the unofficial Christmas truce reached the commanders of the Allied and German armies, they were not amused. Orders were issued to prevent such a truce from happening again, as well as orders for raids and attacks along the line. High command wanted their soldiers to show "offensive spirit" and aggression. They knew that fraternization between soldiers on the two sides only served to underline the similarities between them—especially the similarities of hardships endured in the trenches. To try to keep the level of aggression up, special units were sometimes sent to the front line with the intention of stirring up some action by attacking and irritating the enemy. But despite all the efforts of the high command on both sides, the "live and let live" policy, of which the Christmas truces were just one example, continued along the Western Front throughout the war.

IN THE TRENCHES

The experience of daily life in the trenches depended largely on whether a soldier found himself on an "active" or "quiet" section of the front line. In active areas, the two sides were constantly antagonizing each other with snipers' bullets, raids, mortar shells, and bombs. Life in these sectors of the front line was difficult, dangerous, and wearing on the nerves, and casualties could be high. In "quiet" sectors, life was safer but often monotonous, revolving around some kind of daily routine.

A typical day would start at dawn with the order "Stand To," when guard would be kept in case of any attack or aggression from the enemy. The order "Stand Down" signaled that it was time for breakfast. Food was vitally important for the men on the front line, and rations were usually plentiful. Water came from water carts or from local farms or pumps. Many soldiers slept during the day, as there was more activity during the night. But others did jobs during the day such as repairing trenches, laying down duckboards, or digging dugouts. Lunch was the main meal of the day, after which there could be more duties, called "fatigues," or guard duty or sleep. Dinner was followed by "Stand To" as dusk fell, and then as the order to "Stand Down" came, work started for the night. Nighttime was when patrols went out into No Man's Land to lay wire or to cut wire in preparation for an attack, to assist the wounded, or to collect dead bodies for burial if possible. It was also a time to try to spy on the enemy and to complete work on the trenches that could not safely be done during the day.

Even in "quiet" sectors, life in the trenches was hardly comfortable. Many men put on a brave face in their letters home, and a few positively enjoyed the danger, but for many the experience was intolerable and pointless. One artillery officer wrote to his wife in 1916: "Charming life this is. Both sides bury themselves in mudholes and peep at each other through slits in the earth. Occasionally one side or the other has a bombardment which consists of blowing off £10,000 worth of ammunition and killing no men. Then they retire to their holes to lick their sores like two dogs after a fight."

RIGHT *The trenches were almost constantly wet and muddy, despite pumping and bailing devices.*

? EVENT IN QUESTION

Why did men put up with the conditions on the front?

The trenches were unhealthy places. The constant mud and water—sometimes waist-deep—gave many soldiers "trench foot," a disease in which the feet literally rotted inside the boots. In "active" sectors, the sound of gunfire and explosions, lack of sleep, and constant danger left many men with broken nerves, a condition that became known as "shell-shock." In the filthy conditions of the trenches, diseases such as dysentery and "trench fever" were also widespread. So why did men put up with such conditions? Partly, the strict military discipline of the army gave them little or no choice, and partly, shared experiences created an intense comradery between the men in the front line that helped them carry on in the face of adversity. High command also tried to keep spirits up by giving soldiers warm clothes, adequate food, rations of alchohol, and leave from the trenches when possible.

COMMANDERS AND COMMANDED

While the ordinary soldiers of the British, French, and German armies coped with the day-to-day realities of life in the trenches, their commanders lived in safety and some luxury, well behind the front lines. The British commander-in-chief, General Haig, was based for much of the war at a chateau near Montreuil in northern France. There he lived in splendor, certainly compared to the conditions endured by the men under his command. Most afternoons he went for a ride on his immaculately groomed horse, on roads specially sanded to keep the horse's hooves from slipping. War correspondent Philip Gibbs frequently witnessed Haig setting off for his daily ride and could not help contrasting what he saw with the horrors of the front line, roughly 56 miles (90 km) away: "One often saw the commander-in-chief [Haig] starting for an afternoon ride, a fine figure, nobly mounted, with two

BELOW *Members of the German high command relax in comfort after a good dinner.*

ADCs [aides-de-camp] and an escort of Lancers. A pretty sight, with fluttering pennons [flags] on their lances and horses groomed to the last hair. It was prettier than the real thing up in the Salient [Ypres] or beyond the Somme, where dead bodies lay on upheaved earth among ruins and slaughtered trees. War at Montreuil was quite a pleasant experience for elderly generals. . . ."

British Prime Minister David Lloyd George wrote that "the solicitude with which most generals in high places (there were honorable exceptions) avoided personal jeopardy is one of the debatable novelties of modern warfare. . . ." It is certainly true that much of the high command had little idea about the true conditions in the trenches and made plans of attack with little conception of the realities for the men on the ground. However, some generals did expose themselves to danger and were prepared to stand up for their men if they thought a plan was faulty. It could also be argued that it was necessary for commanders to stay away from the front line in order to be best positioned to receive communications and to try to piece together a broader picture of what was going on, away from the heat of battle.

? EVENT IN QUESTION

Why was high command so out of touch with the realities of life on the front line?

The stark contrasts in living conditions and the dangers endured between those in command and those being commanded did not go unnoticed by the men at the front. As the war developed, many ordinary front line soldiers began to feel more sympathy and affinity with their enemy counterparts than with their own, distant commanders. As one British soldier said, "When one is in the front line one cannot help having a fairly deep sympathy for the wretched fellow in the other front line across no-man's-land; one knows that he is going through just as many dangers and discomforts, and that he is simply carrying out the orders of some general whose dangers and discomforts are infinitely less, and the hatred you both have towards these generals breeds a common sympathy that is irresistible. . . ."

DESERTION

For some soldiers, life on the front line became so unbearable that they simply ran away. This was known as desertion, and in the British army it was punishable by death. Another means of leaving the front line was a self-inflicted wound—in the foot, for example. However, this was risky because if the wound was proved to be self-inflicted, it also became a crime punishable by death. During World War I, the British army sentenced 3,080 of its own soldiers to death for charges including desertion, cowardice, sleeping while on duty, and disobedience. Of these, 346 executions were carried out by firing squads, with the remainder mostly sentenced to hard labor. It is likely that at least some who were judged to be "cowards" were simply suffering from acute shell-shock and were unable to continue. Australia refused to allow any of its troops to be executed, despite protests from

General Haig. There were far fewer death sentences in either the French or German armies, although the French army suffered the most serious mutinies of the war.

MUTINY

The French mutinies happened during the Nivelle Offensive (see page 23) as soon as it became clear that, despite Nivelle's promises, the attack was a failure. Although supposed to last no longer than 48 hours, and despite huge casualties, Nivelle insisted that the offensive continue. While no front-line troops mutinied, when ordered back to the front, many French soldiers simply refused to go. The mutinies continued throughout May 1917 and into early June. Nivelle was dismissed in mid-May and replaced by General Pétain, who began restoring order.

❓ EVENT IN QUESTION

What provoked the French army to mutiny in 1917?

The French mutinies were serious, coming as they did at such a critical point of the war. Many politicians were deeply suspicious of the protesting soldiers, suspecting a revolutionary plot. But it seems that the mutinous troops had simply had enough of being ordered to do the impossible—and going on strike was the only way they could express their grievances. There was certainly no intention to allow the Germans to win the war as a result of the mutinies.

Pétain listened to the soldiers' grievances but also imposed military discipline. In all, 3,427 French soldiers were court-martialed, and 554 were sentenced to death. Of these, 49 were actually shot. General Haig considered this too lenient and remarked that "Pétain ought to have shot 2,000." At the same time, Pétain visited his troops and made various promises. Conditions in the trenches would be improved, and a system of leave and rest would be set up. There would be no more major attacks on the scale of the Nivelle Offensive; instead, the French would wait for "the Americans and the tanks." In accordance with these promises, Pétain instituted a more defensive policy along the French front line. Amazingly, the Germans failed to realize what was going on in the French army and to capitalize on its disarray.

The End of the War

The attack on the Marne (the Second Battle of the Marne) that formed the last part of Ludendorff's Offensive (see page 27) came to an end on July 17, 1918. Ludendorff now knew that he had lost too many men to be able to make up his losses, and he called off plans for another offensive in Flanders. This was the beginning of the end for the Germans.

THE ALLIED ADVANCE

BELOW *A group of American soldiers pose with a German machine gun captured during the St. Mihiel offensive in 1918.*

The Allies had suffered greatly during Ludendorff's Offensive, but they had also learned valuable lessons. Now united under the French Chief of Staff, Field Marshal Ferdinand Foch, they began to plan a series of attacks to drive the Germans back. These attacks were successful partly because of new tactics such as surprising the enemy, large-scale use of tanks (as seen at Cambrai), and better coordination between tanks, infantry, and artillery. Communications were also slightly improved thanks to the use of radio sets (see page 38). But the overwhelming factor in the Allies' favor was the Americans. The number of American troops arriving on the Western Front by 1918 was deeply disturbing for the Germans and sapped the already low morale of the German soldiers.

The Allies launched the first of their counteroffensives on August 8. It was spearheaded by Canadian and Australian troops near Amiens and was an immediate success. Ludendorff wrote in his diary that "August the 8th was a black day for the German Army in the history of this war." Thousands of Germans surrendered with little resistance. The counteroffensive rolled on, and by September 9, the Allies had recovered all of the ground lost during Ludendorff's Offensive. Disillusionment about the war had spread to Germany too, where people on the home front were starving as a result of the Allied blockade of Germany. When new recruits arrived on the front line, they were accused of hurting Germany by prolonging the war.

Nevertheless, the Germans did not give up easily, and the fighting continued through September at St. Mihiel and in the Meuse-Argonne region, where there were heavy Allied casualties. On September 29, Ludendorff finally admitted to the Kaiser (German king) that he thought the war was lost. The German government wrote to President Wilson requesting a truce, but when the reply came the terms were considered too harsh. Ludendorff began to reconsider his position and demanded that the war should continue. It was, however, too late.

? EVENT IN QUESTION

General Erich von Ludendorff (1865–1937)

Together with General Paul von Hindenburg, Ludendorff had virtually controlled Germany since 1916. After that date, these two men had made all of the major German decisions of the war, including those to resume unrestricted submarine warfare and to launch the Ludendorff Offensive. Ludendorff risked everything when he ordered these attacks on the Western Front in 1918. On September 28, 1918, when it became clear that they—and he —had failed, Ludendorff fell into a hysterical rage and collapsed, although reports of these events were later denied. But Germany still had a relatively determined army in strong defensive positions occupying more land than before the war, and the Allies were not yet advancing. Although outright victory was unlikely, a skilled diplomat may have been able to negotiate favorable peace terms for Germany. But Ludendorff was no diplomat. He had fought for victory for Germany, and now that it was out of his grasp, he started to look for ways to divert the blame away from himself.

CONFLICT IN GERMANY

When Ludendorff met with the Kaiser on September 29, 1918, he requested that a new democratic government should be formed in Germany. It would be up to the members of this new government to negotiate a truce with the Allies, and the shame of Germany's defeat would fall squarely on the civilian government and not on the army. Despite having been in effective control of Germany for the previous two years, Ludendorff made the following outrageous statement: "I have asked His Majesty to bring those people into the government who are largely responsible that things have turned out as they have. We shall therefore see these gentlemen enter the ministries, and they must now make the peace which has to be made. They must now eat the soup they have ladled out to us."

TOWARD A TRUCE

The new German government based its request for peace on a document drawn up in January 1918 by the American president, Woodrow Wilson. It was known as the "Fourteen Points" because it listed 14 terms on which an honorable peace and new world order could be based. But when the Allies replied to the German request, the German government considered the terms too harsh.

BELOW *Allied troops on the bank of the St. Quentin Canal in September 1918.*

Ludendorff, who had by then recovered his nerve, began to demand that the Germans should continue to fight for victory. The tension between a government trying to negotiate peace terms and a general trying to continue the war became too much. On October 26, Ludendorff was forced to resign.

Meanwhile, the fighting continued across northern France. At the end of September, Allied troops approached the Hindenburg Line and took the St. Quentin Canal. Throughout October, the Allies continued to push the Germans back, although casualties remained high.

The Allied leaders met in Paris to discuss a truce. While the British and French were mostly in favor of bringing an end to the fighting, American commander General John Pershing thought that the Allies should force the Germans into an unconditional surrender. This was not to happen, however. On November 8, in a special train in the Forest of Compiegne near Paris, the Allied leader General Foch met with a German delegation. After days of negotiation, the truce was signed at 5:00 A.M. on November 11, 1918. Fighting stopped on the Western Front at 11:00 A.M. the same day.

? EVENT IN QUESTION

Was the German army "stabbed in the back"?

The German army marched home from the Western Front looking for all intents and purposes like an undefeated force. Indeed, many people in Germany believed that the army had not been defeated in the field, but that it had been betrayed by the German government. Of course, shifting the blame for defeat was Ludendorff's intention, and the rumor that the army had been "stabbed in the back" by the civilian government suited his purposes perfectly. In fact, if the army was stabbed in the back by anyone, it was by its own commander. Nevertheless, the legend that the army had been betrayed by civilian socialists, Jews, and pacifists continued to circulate, and this lie eventually came to contribute to the rise to power of Adolf Hitler, and the start of the next catastrophic war.

RIGHT *The end of the war is greeted with joy and relief by the French people. A wounded Canadian soldier stands among the crowd.*

WAR GUILT

The truce signed on November 11 imposed many conditions on the defeated Germans. Within two weeks, the Germans had to evacuate all captured territory, as well as Alsace and Lorraine, which became French territories once again. They also had to hand over vast amounts of equipment—enough to ensure that the fighting could not continue—to release all prisoners of war, and to pay war reparations.

Of the nations involved in the fighting on the Western Front, only the U.S. profited economically from the war. Britain, France, and Germany all had huge war debts, and in addition, France had suffered terrible devastation in the areas where battles had raged. All of the participating nations on the Western Front had suffered thousands upon thousands of casualties, and the sense of loss and grief would take a long time to heal. It is not surprising, then, that many people in the victorious countries thought that Germany should be made to pay for the war.

Who won the war?

The simple answer to this question is the Allies, who were able to dictate terms and conditions to the defeated Germans. But as time went on, many people in Germany came to believe that the war had ended in a draw between the two sides, with the balance of power shared equally. No part of the German homeland had been occupied during the war, and Germany was left with its industry intact, although its economy, like those of Britain and France, was in ruins. France had reclaimed its lost territories of Alsace and Lorraine, but its priority remained security against invasion from its still-powerful neighbor. Britain had gained little or nothing from the war, while the U.S. emerged from the war with a new position as the biggest creditor nation in the world.

Negotiations for peace began in January 1919 in Paris. Although 32 nations were represented, the decisions were effectively made by just four men (the "Council of Four"): British prime minister David Lloyd George, French president Georges Clemenceau, American president Woodrow Wilson, and Italian premier Vittorio Orlando. The Germans were not included in the negotiations. The Treaty of Versailles was signed on June 28, 1919, in the Hall of Mirrors at the Palace of Versailles. The most controversial part of the Treaty was Article 231, known as the "War Guilt Clause." It forced Germany to accept responsibility for starting the war, and therefore to pay huge war reparations to the Allies. The final figure for these reparations was not decided until 1921. Germany also lost territory in Europe and all of its overseas colonies, its army was reduced in size, recruitment was forbidden, and its fleet was surrendered to Britain.

The German public was outraged by the Treaty of Versailles, and those who had signed it on their behalf became known to many as "the criminals of 1919." Whether or not the Treaty of Versailles was a just settlement, it was viewed in Germany as unreasonably harsh, and it helped the growth of the nationalist movement in Germany. In Britain, a growing belief that the Treaty was too harsh also helped to foster the policy of appeasement toward Germany in the 1930s. The course was set for another war.

BELOW *Makeshift wooden crosses mark the graves of dead American soldiers in 1918.*

Timeline

1914

JUNE 28 Assassination of Archduke Franz Ferdinand and his wife in Sarajevo.

JULY 23 Austria-Hungary issues ultimatum to Serbia.

JULY 28 Austria-Hungary declares war on Serbia.

JULY 30 Russia mobilizes its army.

AUGUST 1 Germany declares war on Russia.

AUGUST 3 Germany declares war on France.

AUGUST 4 German troops invade Belgium.

AUGUST 4 Britain declares war on Germany.

AUGUST 9 First British troops land in France.

AUGUST 20 Germans capture Brussels.

AUGUST 23–24 Battle of Mons.

AUGUST 26 Moltke diverts troops to East Prussia.

SEPTEMBER 2 French government leaves Paris.

SEPTEMBER 4–10 Battle of the Marne.

SEPTEMBER 9 Moltke orders Germans to retreat to River Aisne.

SEPTEMBER 12–18 First Battle of the Aisne.

MID SEPTEMBER–LATE OCTOBER "Race for the Sea."

SEPTEMBER 14 General Erich von Falkenhayn takes over from Moltke.

MID OCTOBER–MID NOVEMBER First Battle of Ypres.

NOVEMBER Construction of trench system begins.

1915

MARCH 10–13 Allied attack at Neuve Chapelle.

APRIL 22 Start of Second Battle of Ypres; Germans use gas on front line for first time.

MAY 7 Sinking of *Lusitania* by German U-boat.

SEPTEMBER 15 First use of gas by Allies at Loos.

DECEMBER 18 General Douglas Haig replaces Sir John French.

DECEMBER 20 Falkenhayn proposes Verdun attack.

1916

FEBRUARY 21 Operation Gericht marks beginning of fighting at Verdun.

JUNE 24 Preliminary bombardment of German lines begins on the Somme.

JULY 1–NOVEMBER 19 Battle of the Somme.

AUGUST 29 Ludendorff and Hindenburg replace Falkenhayn.

SEPTEMBER 15 First use of tanks on the battlefield.

1917

MARCH 16 Start of Operation Alberich as Germans withdraw to Hindenburg Line.

APRIL 6 The U.S. declares war on Germany.

APRIL 9 Battle of Arras starts with capture of Vimy Ridge.

APRIL 16 Nivelle Offensive in the Champagne region.

MAY–JUNE French mutinies.

MAY 15 General Henri Pétain takes over from Nivelle.

JUNE 7 Mines detonated on Messines Ridge.

JULY 17 Preliminary bombardment begins at Ypres.

JULY 31–NOVEMBER 18 Third Battle of Ypres (Passchendaele).

NOVEMBER 20 First successful use of tanks at Battle of Cambrai.

1918
JANUARY Wilson draws up "Fourteen Points."

MARCH 3 Treaty of Brest-Litovsk marks end of war on Eastern Front.

MARCH 21 Operation Michael marks start of Ludendorff's Offensive.

APRIL Ludendorff's second offensive in Flanders.

MAY–JUNE Ludendorff's third offensive in the Aisne.

MAY 28 U.S. troops see action for first time at Cantigny.

JULY Second Battle of the Marne.

AUGUST 8 Allied counter-offensives begin.

SEPTEMBER–NOVEMBER Allied offensives in Meuse-Argonne region.

SEPTEMBER AEF fights as an independent force at St. Mihiel.

SEPTEMBER 29 Allied forces cross St. Quentin Canal.

OCTOBER 9 Allied forces cross Hindenburg Line.

OCTOBER 26 Ludendorff forced to resign.

NOVEMBER 8 Allies meet German armistice delegation in Forest of Compiegne.

NOVEMBER 11 Truce starts at 11:00 A.M.

Glossary

appeasement Foreign policy based on diplomacy and negotiation with hostile states in an attempt to avoid war

armaments Weapons

arms race The "race" beween two opposing nations to accumulate a larger supply of more powerful weapons

Balkans The Balkan States in the southeast part of Europe

blockade The use of military force by one nation to prevent access to an enemy nation's ports or other key supply points

cavalry A regiment of mounted troops

censor Someone who controls the exchange of information, for example in newspapers, personal letters, etc.

Central Powers A term denoting the alliance of Germany and Austria-Hungary during World War I

conscription Mandatory military service

convalescent Someone who is recovering from an illness or injury

court martial A military court in which people are tried according to military law

creeping barrage One of the tactical innovations introduced on the Western Front; the idea was that a wall of shells would fall just ahead of attacking troops in order to neutralize the enemy

delegation A group of people chosen to represent others

democratic government Government that is elected by popular vote

diplomacy Peaceful negotiation between two or more states

draft system In the U.S., the term for conscription

dysentery An infection of the intestine that occurs in areas with poor standards of hygiene

firing squad A group of soldiers whose job is to execute those sentenced to death by shooting

fraternization Association on friendly terms between two people or groups of people

military service Service in one of the armed forces

mobilization The act of preparing for war

munitions Military equipment

mutiny Rebellion against higher command

nationalist Someone who is passionately loyal to his or her own country

pacifist Someone who believes in finding a negotiated settlement rather than resorting to violence and war

periscope A device that uses mirrors to allow someone to see objects that are not in their direct line of vision (for example, over the top of a trench)

reconnaissance The act of obtaining vital information about enemy movements and positions

reparations Compensation

salient A "bulge" into enemy territory of the front line of an attacking force

sniper A marksman who fires at individual enemy soldiers

stalemate A situation in conflict where neither side can make a move

Territorials Members of the Territorial Army, the reserve force of the British Army

trajectory The path taken by an object moving through the air

trench fever An infectious fever caused by the bites of lice

truce An agreement between enemy sides to suspend hostilities

war of attrition A tactic whereby one side hopes to wear its enemy down by inflicting more casualties than the enemy can inflict on it

Further Information

BOOKS

Brown, Malcolm. *The Imperial War Museum Book of the Western Front*. London: Sidgwick and Jackson/IWM, 1994.

Bull, Stephen. *World War I Trench Warfare 1914–16*. Wellingborough: Osprey Publishing, 2002.

Ellis, John. *Eye-Deep in Hell: Trench Warfare in World War I*. Baltimore: John Hopkins University Press, 1989.

Farrar, Martin J. *News from the Front*. Stroud: Sutton Publishing, 1999.

Holmes, Richard. *The Western Front: Ordinary Soldiers and the Defining Battles of World War I*. New York: TV Books, 2000.

Keegan, John. *An Illustrated History of the First World War*. New York: Knopf, 2001.

Macdonald, Lyn. *1914–1918: Voices and Images of the Great War*. New York: Penguin, 1991.

Mosier, John. *The Myth of the Great War*. London: Profile Books, 2002.

Saunders, Anthony. *Weapons of the Trench War 1914–1918*. Stroud: Sutton Publishing, 1999.

Index